SEX ADDICTION

THE COMPLETE GUIDE TO SEX ADDICTION RECOVERY

ROBBIE DYER

CONTENTS

Introduction   v

Sex Addiction Recovery   1
Facing The Addiction   6
Acting Out   10
Wake Up Call   14
Shame Shift   18

©Copyright 2022 by Robbie Dyer
All rights Reserved

ISBN: 978-1-63970-122-3

In no way is it legal to reproduce, duplicate, or transmit any part of this document in either electronic means or in printed format. Recording of this publication is strictly prohibited and any storage of this document is not allowed unless with written permission from the publisher. All rights are reserved.
Respective authors own all copyrights not held by the publisher.

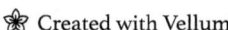 Created with Vellum

INTRODUCTION

My name is Robbie Dyer, and I was once a sex addict. I am extremely passionate about the contents of this book because it saved my life. I know exactly what it's like to suffer from sex addiction. I know the feelings of guilt, depression, and frustration after each sex-related episode and how it was destroying my life. I know what it's like to be in a hurry to make that call, log on to that site I knew well, have low self-esteem, and have the feeling of learned helplessness because you have tried seemingly everything out there. Sex addiction was the worst thing of my life. I used to run to my office, lock the door and turn on the computer or make that private call or make that appointment. Thankfully, I was able to overcome it and get my life back on track. My life has transformed since I´ve transformed my life completely and now enjoy a wonderful life free of the things that were destroying my life, helped hundreds of people with similar problems, and even wrote this book, which I hope gets to people who need it.

This book is a compilation of the best of what I've learned to help you overcome sex addiction and be able to build the habits and lifestyle for you to be happy, proud, have great relationships, energetic and confident in yourself, and it contains proven steps and strategies on how to cure yourself once and for all of your sex addiction by giving you a step by step guide that takes you by the hand to cure yourself of this problem which many people face, the truth is that if you haven't been able to cure your addiction to sex is because you haven't changed your associations towards sex addiction, may it be in the form of pornography, strip clubs, prostitutes, massage parlors, phone sex, chat rooms or others.

Sex addiction often interferes with everyday living and causes stress to the family, loved ones, friends, and work environments. Often sex addicts make sex a priority over their work and friendships. Using the concepts, ideas, and techniques contained in this book you'll be able to free yourself from this addiction that destroys lives.

This book´s changed my life, and I am confident that it will change your life if you apply these same strategies.

I wish you the best of luck and want to thank you for downloading this book again. I am here to support you in any way that I can.

SEX ADDICTION RECOVERY

For a large part of clinical history- sex was scrutinized as to whether or not it is actually a type of addiction or just a hormone-related overdrive. The reason being, sex is a very natural act, and over-indulging in it to the point where it creates an imbalance in life- was a sensitive task to ascertain. Bringing it out as psychological trauma and its adverse effects on society was always an issue of debate.

THROUGH THIS E-BOOK, we will lead you through a process after which you will realize that it is more of a mindset and behavioral shift issue. And once you're aware of it, it isn't a challenging feat to accomplish. With gradual understanding and assessment- anyone can overcome this obstacle that is leaving a hampering effect on the life of those associated and/or connected with it.

FIRST OF ALL, we'll like to clarify that it is not a chronic disease. Instead, it is a condition that combines socio-psychological attitudes- something that can easily be tackled through behavioral and mindset screening. If only one is ready to acknowledge and marginalize this overdrive's side effects, it is rather easier to approach and demystify towards resolution.

IN LAYMAN WORDS, sexual addiction is an obsession or overindulgence in one or more sexual acts- where it entails deteriorating effects on other facets of life- these normally include the following areas, which are discussed underneath:

SOCIAL: In strictly religious terms- sex is a sacred phenomenon that is marginally applied for reproduction. In recreational and relaxation terms- it can entail a soothing effect. However, its overindulgence can sometimes have a social impact that can create gaps within us and the society that we belong to.

SEXUAL ADDICTION typically triggers and revolves around obsession and fantasies- following which the addict is driven to overlook the boundaries drawn by civil societies. They view each person in the light of that obsession, and the value structure and moral grounds are severely crushed in such pursuits. This is legally dangerous and socially unethical- it has to be clearly understood before the change is initiated.

MEDICAL: Since sex is a natural phenomenon, it is vital to understand that it consumes valuable energy that can hamper our productivity and potency if it is over-utilized. A massive amount of vital energy is derived from our bodies during, before, and after sex. Therefore, we must avail these climaxes occasionally, when the urge is ripe, and the desire is irrepressible. However, if utilized as an escape or as a casual ritual- it can have unsatisfactory psychological results. It will lose the charm and pleasure derived from it through a repetitive and excessive application.

FINANCIAL: There are registered cases and studies- where people have lost a humungous amount of monetary assets in the libertarian pursuits of prostitution, adultery, and porn. Sex addiction can leave people destitute, just like in the case of gambling addiction. It's only a buzz that is acquired and assumed. It is no different than an impulsive splurging of cash without any remorse for consequences and checks and balances. In many cases, people end up tarnishing their image, bringing shame to their families and destabilizing an everyday prosperous life in the chase of a fantasy.

THE DISINTEGRATION OF MORAL, Marital, and Professional grounds are also associated aspects of similar practices.

NOW WE'LL micro-manage a bit about the symptoms of Sexual Addiction and find whether or not you are part of it.

OBSESSION: Sexual addiction initiates with a sexually embedded obsession. It could be part of memory, and it could also be an aftereffect of physical/sexual/verbal abuse. It is an unrealistic mental entanglement with an act or a fantasy about a situation, body part, or relationship disorder that has taken root in the psychology of an addicted person. It can happen to anyone—so no need to feel victimized as a consequence. The point is to take charge and eradicate it from your subconscious- where it actually rehearses and re-emerges over and over, time and again.

COMPULSIVE REPETITION: The state of the joy derived out of sex has an ecstasy memory. It creates repetitive arousal in the mind of the addict. Revisiting and reliving as long as one can, is the prime objective as a consequence. This state of mind invites the addict for back-to-back pleasure. Whereas in reality, it is decreased with the frequency to the point of numbness- when it is hard for anything to be felt but a mere indulgence in the procedure. This state is also often compared to Obsessive-Compulsive Disorder, during which it becomes a necessity for the addict to go through the complete emotion at every cost.

DENIAL: Self-deception is the key aspect of sex addiction. The bliss of sex becomes the sole objective and denies the consequences or side effects of this exercise. Denial to oneself and those who are related and involved in the lifestyle of the addicted person is a normal symptom. You negate the effects of this overindulgence and start feeling entitled and victimized. Self-sympathy and intolerance to the feelings and responses of others are part and parcel of this phase. Such denial can often lead to isolation and shutting oneself away from the regular proceedings of life.

INDIFFERENCE: Another key symptom of sex addiction is negligence, indifference, and ignorance for its adverse and diverse effects. The person becomes oblivious of the responsibilities and obligations for family, relatives, friends, and society. The situations they will have to face and the drama that might occur inside and outside their homes are of little concern. For them, there is that utter gush in their heads of touching the climax and feeling the bliss without any regard for the outcome. As a result, the person loses credibility, and people stop expecting while reciprocating their needs and concerns.

DEFENSE MECHANISM: Now that the addicted person is on the road of accomplishment with frequency- they put full force into action for anything or anyone that suppresses their urges. They want things their way- the way that holds them up for their sexual pursuits. They become less adaptable to change and resist anything that leads them away from their addiction. They try their utmost effort to stay aligned to their acts and fantasies no matter what may hinder their way. They are sidelined and detracted because people living with them have lost hope in their reversion. Likewise, they stay out of the course of anything or any event that keeps their sexual indulgences under threat of extinction.

FACING THE ADDICTION

*B*efore eradicating sex addiction- it is vital to realize that one is facing this addictive sexual condition. It means that to firewall yourself from further damage- one has to establish that the problem is there and that before resolution, one has to register it in his/her mind to overcome it gradually. Moving on to the next phase to fight anxiety and increasing stress level, occurring due to putting a cap on the addiction- is very hard until the problem is registered and defined in the brain.

IN OTHER WORDS, for one to activate the moralistic powers from the core- one must rationalize the decisions- based on which this abstinence is required. Skipping or bypassing this phase put one in a state of chaos- where we are forced to find refuge in that addiction again. On two levels, we have to fight our demons- firstly, to overcome the anxiety, and secondly, to gratify the missing link that creates that odd situation in mind. You sell your soul to the devil- to bail you out for bad.

. . .

THERE IS ONLY one way to combat such casualty is when an ad-hoc approach is applied to overcome this struggle. You may swear that you won't go back to it, but your guilt comes in
to play when you are already halfway through it. You will have to get ready for the fire fighting necessary when the hangover is taking over. We all have personal values that are close to heart and are close to a personal being. They give strength to us in overcoming obstacles and adversaries in the heart and mind- these values are severely tormented and damaged in the process. You push up for giving up before actually screening it. You are let down by yourself in your own eyes, and it is tough to face yourself through this critical scenario.

SO THE BEST is to relax and watch your movie in rewind.

IT ALL BECOMES easy when you start to negotiate with yourself regarding a statement of the problem. Before you try to counter it with full holistic might- you need first to ensure that you have understood, analyzed, and evaluated all aspects of your sexual addiction. You need to be your spectator and observe how it all happens- from arousal to discharge. Finally, you need to mirror yourself properly- investigating and rationalizing the tarnishing impacts it is leaving on the other aspects of your life and those associated with you.

THERE ARE many self-help and rehab programs to escort you through the recovery process, but why does it come back to haunt you in solitude? It is a different ball game altogether. This is where it all starts- self-actualization and catching yourself red-handed and accepting that there is a situation that requires you to step in and take charge. It only becomes easy when you have adjusted the sail according to your conditions.

FURTHERMORE, when you come out clean- it helps your partner to understand your condition more crucially and critically before you both can easily manage it. Making half-hearted attempts and putting a cushion under to ease your scenario is just another way of losing your hope to demystify the action orientation required- to respect your scenario. Problems are best solved- when you realize that there is a problem. Statement of it in a written form is even more so effective. It's like approaching it both objectively and subjectively- your desire and drive are easily controlled when quality and quantity are measured and covered. It's not about high or less frequency- it is about the dire consequences and the current embarrassment of witnessing the scene.

THE STEPS of establishing the sexual addiction for recovery involves overcoming:

COMPLACENCY:
Denial goes a step ahead when the addict thinks that it is fine to keep it all closeted. Waiting for a messiah and for things to fall from the sky at the right places is the best way to slip into complacency. Instead, the truth is needed to come out and share your problems with those who matter to you. And once they watch your back or cover it up- things will start rolling better for you.

. . .

Tweaked Pragmatism:

Associating your practices as normal or considering that it is okay to associate yourself with similar groups is another way to stagnate your progress. Keep yourself away from such influences- whether they are online or offline. Such a company will make you sluggish or might push your addiction to the next level. Cut all such ties, and you'll feel better.

Reclusion:

Isolation occurs when the addict becomes selfish in their being. Regardless of your partner's feelings or lack of respect for the relationship, you keep moving forward towards self-destructive lust. You think that these addictions as secrets will not harm or affect your partner or your bond, and you keep moving towards the darker zones.

ACTING OUT

*A*ddiction is, more importantly, a mode of thinking and a behavioral trait. It provides the necessary firewall to the addicts to overcome their anxiety. It is their ever-ready solution to lean on for normalizing their nervous system. And going without addiction is making them vulnerable to plausible and empirical thinking. So when they look at life without the context of addiction, they find boredom and chalk out brand new ways to fulfill and satisfy it—feeding their urge while giving themselves ample reasons to fall between victimization and entitlement.

TO COUNTER this phase- they have fits, which is also known as acting-out in addiction terminology. Such displays of tantrums and temper are their necessary mechanism to counteract the threat they face as an opportunity cost of their addiction. This is a necessary mode of venting, exhausting, and touches a level of brainstorming- where their addiction is exorcised out, as they go and feel light while confessing, defending, denying, and supporting their addiction, all at once. They show remorse and anger they have for and against this addiction, and they can even burst into tears ultimately when they know it cannot be fulfilled or satisfied the easy ways they wanted before. Although deep down in their hearts, they know it is bad for them, guilt paves the way inside their being- making them regret each time they leaned on their sex addiction habits.

IT MAY SOUND SUBJECTIVE, but it is in a way necessary for the addict to feel heard and vomit it all out through the anguish and pain they are suffering through. Your approach, too, can be radical, and the fits can be unpredictable without regard for time and place. But this is mandatory- so it can fill the gaps required to face the consequences towards recovery.

RECOVERY IS a painful act and phases out gradually- you have to undo all the damage while controlling it. It is challenging and quite volatile to handle. The mercuric behavior before and after acting out can have severe wounds on the soul, so it is only fair to ensure a safe setting for yourself- when and where you feel the strength of emotion overwhelming your cognitive response and senses in general. Take charge and unwind it.

FOLLOWING ARE the two routes you might adopt psychologically to challenge your binge:

VICTIMIZATION: Self-sympathy is the best refuge for an addict to dive into despair. They constantly reassure themselves that it is all about being the victim. Sometimes they blame circumstances, and at times they blame other people. In many cases, the addicts are victimized in physical/sexual abuse, but that's not a reason solid enough to spoil one's life.

HOPELESSNESS AND PESSIMISM are one enemy of human progress- we all slide in it, but to move on in life and divorcing our past miseries, we have to think logically and productively to grow on towards better.

AS A SEX ADDICT, you have to reassure and remind yourself that life is not a bed of roses but giving others the power to spoil your life against the pain that some people have inflicted on you- is not indeed a reason, valid enough to spoil your life. It is good and bad in this world, and sometimes anyone can fall into the trap of wrong timing and, by chance, get stuck in a wrong situation. But there is always tomorrow, and the only way to survive is to heal the wounds yourself and grow stronger. You must have heard the Kelly Clarkson song "What doesn't kill you, make you stronger," and it is so true about sex addiction recovery.

ENTITLEMENT: The very other end of the spectrum of the same problem is Entitlement. It is the opposite in the sense that instead of hopelessness, it lets you glide in complacency- a make-believe scenario that all is fine and that sooner than later, everything will fix on its own. You start believing in the unreasonably miraculous powers of the time.

ESCAPE from reality is the other name of addiction. And returning to innocence and reality is the real way to recovery. It is easy to slide into self-denial about your life and the people associated with it. But in truth, it is only a defense mechanism so that you can continue your addiction without ascertaining the critical state of your personal life affairs.

IN SOME WAYS, Entitlement is even worse than victimization. The reason being- you are blinded by your willpower to evaluate and analyze your conditions in a factual manner. You deceive yourself with all positivity. You take addiction as a break from your tiresome chores and that it is not (in any way) rampaging your social relationships and marital bond.

ALL IN ALL, acting-out is a sensitive phase that should pass as soon as possible on the road of recovery. It should have a slow persuading power to activate your inner sense of well-being, integrity, and sincerity for your good cause. It has to be maneuvered through and not manipulated- you need to talk yourself out of it and provide enough rationality- while its benefits will derive for you over time.

WAKE UP CALL

Addiction may be acquired, adapted, or culminated as a bad habit over the years. And may also take a lot of time to get rid of it. Yet, it becomes easier to recover when the support structure or system of the addicted is suddenly jolted- preemptively or suddenly. This is commonly known as a Wake-Up Call, when the addict suddenly hits the bottom line and realizes that he/she has nothing to hold on to, except the addiction and that too is losing its charm and charisma without the presence of the support structure, to switch back on or lean on to.

ANY PERSONAL CATASTROPHE can lead to this wake-up call. Addictive behavior can face a dilemma from any or multiple aspects when either one of these is no more on your side.

TIME: Time is the most vital resource of modern life. In many cases, it is more worthy than money- one can fix monetary loss, but the loss made in terms of opportunity cost of time can never be revived or retrieved no matter what.

. . .

TIME CAN REPRESENT the personal or professional phase when one realizes suddenly that it is too late to put a cap on the addictive behavior or habits. It could be a sudden vacuum felt as a consequence of extended sex addiction. You feel all that has been missed during the time that got wasted in addiction. Time is certainly a meaningful barometer of one's success or failure, and it is silent cancer just like it is a healer. It is the way to verify progress or deceleration both on professional and personal fronts.

ENERGY: Youth is a gift, particularly when it comes to sex addiction. It turns out when it is overused or abused. In both cases, addicts chase their buzz to act out their fantasies. Erectile Dysfunction and/or Menopause are both indicators of diminishing energies. Sex is one area, which, if covered evenly, can give us pleasures all our lives- sex addicts face the opposite crisis with overindulgence. The same practices, which once retained vigor, become meaningless and derogatory if your body doesn't respond to addictive acts. Such sexual disorders and dysfunction ahead of time are great wake-up calls and can help in fast recovery from addictive behavior if taken care of immediately.

FINANCES: Finances are the most tangible and evident of the wake-up calls. Compulsive prostitution and pornographic splurging of cash can make one hit bottom. It's upfront and hits right on the face when suddenly an addict doesn't produce income and finds themselves struggling with finances. If you're still with a family and not facing isolation- it is good to recover fast and get back on track. If you're alone and living on a makeshift arrangement, it is better to focus more on your productivity and help you get out of addiction and dire straits.

RELATIONSHIPS: Friends, family, relatives, and strangers in general. A prosperous and enterprising soul is evident from a distance, and likewise, a person clinging on to addictive behavior is also visible from far. People can easily feel dark circles under their eyes, anxiety, and lack of concentration we interact with daily. Some of these bonds can help us grow out of addictive behavior, and some move on with their lives- leaving us behind. Loss of non-addict friend circle, moving away from family, and lack of zest to interact with strangers- all such elusive and reclusive behavior can count towards such wake-up calls. Sex addicts are always looking out for people to accompany them around to the point where they have to pay for sex and/or a drink to have a pep talk.

HEALTH: Last but not least- health is the real wealth. Our life revolves around it, and only when it starts deteriorating- the warning signs start lingering around our psyche. STD (Sexually Transmitted Disease) is the biggest threat for sex addicts- under the influence of other addictions such as drugs and alcohol, addicts stop caring for precautions and find themselves in fatal chronic diseases. Contriving HIV or a host of other diseases is a very common possibility, and in many cases, the conditions are irreversible. Suddenly, one fine day you realize that you are reaching the dead end of your life- nothing to look forward to, as your journey is coming to an end. Highly prosperous people have fallen prey to this behavior- despite being extremely rich and famous. "Philadelphia" is also a wonderful movie to take pointers from. Better hurry and take charge of your health, or else your life may be at stake.

SHAME SHIFT

*S*hame is good and bad. Shame in its positivity is conscience, in its negative form is ignorance, and its neutral form is acquired from external resources according to the value structure we subscribe to. All that is inculcated in our psyche through our society.

IN AN ADDICTIVE BEHAVIOR, we become numb to the positivity of conscience, and we roll over our integrity, sincerity, ego, and self-esteem. We topple the neutral paths and dive towards the negativity where we atrociously follow the path of indifference to the agendas of life and others- in the context of how they reciprocate with us.

THIS SHAME ROAD map is normally crafted through our childhood during our upbringing from our parents. If our family lives were less than ideal for some reason, we are then devoid of its existence, and we struggle to train our brains to live by it.

. . .

This behavioral and mindset shift requires a lot of perseverance and endurance towards the road of recovery. We don't know what we don't know, and to activate this addictive behavioral shift towards steadfastness and normalization of our lives- we need to understand the "Best Practices for Recovery" and how they can have adverse and diverse effects, in helping us out of our sex addiction and ultimately permanent recovery.

You can exercise these as much as you want to put your recovery plan in effect:

Start your day with zest and positivity for life with a motivational subscription on social media that can inject optimism into your routine thinking.

Try to meditate several times a day- reflecting upon the positive outcomes of staying away from sex addiction.

Put a full stop on your self-destructive addictive behavioral drive and start enforcing the goodness of recovery habits with immediate effect.

Focus and don't let your mind wander away towards addictive rituals. Concentrate and be alert and meaningful about your mental presence

. . .

ENFORCE your new positive practice with full mental and emotional might- let your intuition come to play to let you have a grip over your feelings.

SHARE your secrets with your partner- and give them access to your email and social media accounts and passwords. Put parenting filters and keep your partners in a loop to revive trust and rebounding the lost touch. Share your credit card bills to avoid porn-site transactions.

DON'T DISSUADE, deceive or be a pathological liar. Be open, honest, and smart enough to know your priorities and preferences, with how each action or verbal signal of yours will reflect on your life. Let your life be seen-through by anyone, share your happiness, and don't be an introvert when it comes to living with your guilt or shame.

SOCIALIZE AND DON'T BE an outcast. Participate in mixers, events, and community service, where it is easy to interact with normal zealous people. Who has a proactive approach to life?

HAVE AN OUTGOING LIFESTYLE, work out, or visit the green pastures regularly. Join a gym if it may de-stress your anxiety or yoga or Pilates or cross fitness programs online/offline.

APPRECIATE LIFE and feel good about your life overall- enjoy the progress and relish the recovery by rewarding yourself materially. Shopping, eating out, and a visit to a disco can be fine for your brain cultivation towards prosperity.

Support and help those in need, even if it is just about feeding animals or helping your kids with the homework. You will love the payback that you will feel in their eyes. Support with ingenuity and unconditional generosity without expecting anything in return.

Thus, recovery from sex addiction is rather a mindset shift. Understanding the addictive behavior and facing the scars will help you understand and train your brain towards healing and holding on to it forever. Soon it will become part of your lifestyle and mental outlook. As a result, you will find life more rewarding and will then onwards put in every effort to live it fully.

The End.

www.ingramcontent.com/pod-product-compliance
Lightning Source LLC
LaVergne TN
LVHW021749060526
838200LV00052B/3554